First World War
and Army of Occupation
War Diary
France, Belgium and Germany

15 DIVISION
Divisional Troops
Divisional Trench Mortar Batteries
1 July 1916 - 8 February 1919

WO95/1924/3

The Naval & Military Press Ltd
www.nmarchive.com
Published in association with The National Archives

Published by

The Naval & Military Press Ltd

Unit 10 Ridgewood Industrial Park,
Uckfield, East Sussex,
TN22 5QE England
Tel: +44 (0) 1825 749494

www.naval-military-press.com
www.nmarchive.com

This diary has been reprinted in facsimile from the original. Any imperfections are inevitably reproduced and the quality may fall short of modern type and cartographic standards.

© **Crown Copyright**
Images reproduced by permission of The National Archives, London, England, 2015.

Contents

Document type	Place/Title	Date From	Date To
Heading	WO95/1924/3		
Heading	15th Division 15th Divl Trench Mortar Bty. Aug 1916-Mar 1919		
Heading	War Diary of 15th Divn Medium T.M. Batteries. 1-7-16 To 31-7-16		
War Diary	Hohen Zollern	01/07/1916	01/07/1916
War Diary	Hullnch & Purics	02/07/1916	23/07/1916
War Diary	Monchy Cayeux	24/07/1916	25/07/1916
War Diary	Vacquerie	26/07/1916	26/07/1916
War Diary	Mezerolles	27/07/1916	27/07/1916
War Diary	Boisbergues	28/07/1916	30/07/1916
War Diary	Boudon	31/07/1916	31/07/1916
Heading	War Diary of 15th Divnl Trench Mortars. From 1st September, 1916 to 30 September, 1916. Volume Number. 3.		
Heading	15th Divisional Artillery. 15th Divisional Trench Mortar Officer August 1916		
Heading	War Diary of 15th Divnl Trench Mortars From 1st August. 1916 to 31st August, 1916 Volume Number 7		
War Diary	Boudon	01/08/1916	01/08/1916
War Diary	Bavatincourt	02/08/1916	04/08/1916
War Diary	Albert	05/08/1916	30/09/1916
War Diary		25/09/1916	06/10/1916
Heading	War Diary of 15th Div. Trench Mortar 1st October. 1916 to 31st October, 1916 Volume No. 4		
War Diary	St Gratien	01/10/1916	08/10/1916
War Diary	O.G.I. East of Lcsars.	09/10/1916	31/10/1916
Heading	War Diary. of 15th Div. T. Brigade. From 1st November, 1916-30th November, 1916. Volume 5		
War Diary	La Sars.	01/11/1916	04/11/1916
War Diary	Becourt	08/11/1916	30/11/1916
Heading	War Diary of 15th Divisional Trench Mortar Batteries		
War Diary Miscellaneous	Becourt	01/12/1916	31/12/1916
War Diary	Becourt La Sars	01/01/1917	20/01/1917
War Diary	Peata Wood	21/01/1917	25/01/1917
War Diary	La Sars	26/01/1917	30/01/1917
Heading	War Diary of 15th Divisional Trench Mortar Batteries. For Month of February 1917. Volume XX		
War Diary		01/02/1917	10/02/1917
War Diary		06/02/1917	11/02/1917
War Diary		05/02/1917	28/02/1917
War Diary		26/02/1917	27/02/1917
Miscellaneous	War Diary of 15th Div. T. Ms. From 1st March 1917-To 31st March 1917 Volume IX		
War Diary	Arras	01/03/1917	31/03/1917
War Diary	Arras	23/03/1917	29/03/1917
Heading	War Diary of 15th D.T. No. Volume 4 From 1st April 1917, 30th April, 1917		
War Diary		01/04/1917	30/04/1917

Heading	War Diary of 15th Divisional Trench Mortar Batteries. From 1st May. 1917 to 31st May, 1917 Volume 5.		
War Diary	In The Field	01/05/1917	31/05/1917
Heading	War Diary of 15th Divisional Trench Mortar Batteries. From 1st June, 1917 To 30th June 1917. Volume 6		
War Diary	Monchel	01/06/1917	16/06/1917
War Diary	Teneur	17/06/1917	17/06/1917
War Diary	Tontes	18/06/1917	18/06/1917
War Diary	Steenbecque	19/06/1917	20/06/1917
War Diary	Steenvoorde	21/06/1917	21/06/1917
War Diary	Watou	22/06/1917	24/06/1917
War Diary	Ypres	24/06/1917	24/06/1917
War Diary	Watou	25/06/1917	28/06/1917
War Diary	Vlamertinghe	29/06/1917	30/06/1917
Heading	War Diary of 15th Divisional Trench Mortar Batteries Volume 7 From 1st July 1917 to 31st July 1917		
War Diary	Ypres	01/07/1917	31/07/1917
Heading	War Diary of 15th Divisional Trench Mortar Batteries. From 1st August 1917. To 31st August 1917 Volume 8		
War Diary	Ypres	01/08/1917	31/08/1917
Heading	War Diary of 15th Divisional Trench Mortar Batteries. (Volume 9.) From 1/9/17 To 30/9/17		
War Diary	Watou	01/09/1917	01/09/1917
War Diary	Noordpeene	02/09/1917	03/09/1917
War Diary	Wormhoudt	02/09/1917	03/09/1917
War Diary	Cassel Wormhoudt	04/09/1917	05/09/1917
War Diary	Harbarcq	06/09/1917	07/09/1917
War Diary	Fampoux	08/09/1917	08/09/1917
War Diary	Athies	09/09/1917	30/09/1917
War Diary		10/09/1917	30/09/1917
War Diary		14/09/1917	30/09/1917
War Diary	War Diary of 15th Divisional Trench Mortar Batteries. From 1st October 1917. To 31st October, 1917		
War Diary	Roeux And Monchy	01/10/1917	31/10/1917
War Diary	Roeux & Monchy	01/11/1917	30/11/1917
War Diary	War Diary of 15th Divisional Trench Mortar Brigade (Volume 12) From 1st December 1917. to 31st December 1917		
War Diary	Roeux	01/12/1917	31/12/1917
War Diary	Roeux	01/01/1918	04/01/1918
War Diary	Duisans	05/01/1918	05/01/1918
War Diary	Ligny St Flochel	06/01/1918	19/01/1918
War Diary	Duisans	20/01/1918	24/01/1918
War Diary	Blangy	24/01/1918	24/01/1918
War Diary	Duisans	25/01/1918	31/01/1918
Heading	War Diary of 15th Divisional Trench Mortar Brigade Volume 14 From 1st February 1916 To 1st March 1918		
War Diary	Duisans	01/02/1918	06/02/1918
War Diary	Arras-Monchyle Preux	07/02/1918	28/02/1918
Heading	15th Divisional Artillery. 15th Divisional Trench Mortar Brigade March 1918		
War Diary	Monchy	01/03/1918	14/03/1918
Heading	War Diary of 15th Divisional Trench Mortar Brigade. (Volume 15.) From 1st March 1918. to 31st March 1918		
War Diary	Monchy	18/03/1918	31/03/1918

Heading	15th Divisional Artillery War Diary 15th Divisional Trench Mortar Brigade. April 1918		
Heading	15th Divisional Artillery War Diary 15th Divisional Trench Mortar Brigade. (Volume 16) From 1st April 1918 To 30th April 1918		
War Diary	Arras	01/04/1918	30/04/1918
Heading	War Diary of 15th Divisional Trench Mortar Brigade. (Volume 17.) From 1st May 1918 To 31st May 1918		
War Diary	Arras	01/05/1918	31/05/1918
Heading	War Diary of 15th Divisional Trench Mortar Brigade (Volume 18.) From 1st June 1918. To 30th June 1918		
War Diary		01/06/1918	30/06/1918
Heading	War Diary of 15th Divisional Trench Mortar Brigade. (Volume 19.) From 1st July 1918 To 31st July 1918		
War Diary	Arras	01/07/1918	15/07/1918
War Diary	Aubigny	16/07/1918	17/07/1918
War Diary	Brenoville	18/07/1918	19/07/1918
War Diary	Verberie Vaux-Moulin Coeuvres	20/07/1918	31/07/1918
War Diary		27/07/1918	31/07/1918
Heading	War Diary of 15th Divisional Trench Mortar Brigade From 1st August 1918 To 31st August 1918 (Volume 20)		
War Diary	Coeuvres	01/08/1918	06/08/1918
War Diary	Houvin-Houvigneul	07/08/1918	18/08/1918
War Diary	Arras	19/08/1918	31/08/1918
Heading	War Diary. of 15th Divisional Trench Mortar Brigade (Volume 21) From 1st September 1918. To 30th September 1918		
War Diary	Wancourt	01/09/1918	04/09/1918
War Diary	Arras	05/09/1918	05/09/1918
War Diary	Hersin	06/09/1918	07/09/1918
War Diary	Noyelles	08/09/1918	08/09/1918
War Diary	Loos & Hulluch Sectors.	09/09/1918	30/09/1918
Heading	War Diary of 15th Divisional T.M. Bde. From 1/10/18 to 31/10/18 Volume 22		
War Diary	Loos	01/10/1918	04/10/1918
War Diary	Vendin	05/10/1918	14/10/1918
War Diary	Meuchin	15/10/1918	16/10/1918
War Diary	Newville	17/10/1918	17/10/1918
War Diary	Nouveau-Jev	18/10/1918	18/10/1918
War Diary	Genech	19/10/1918	19/10/1918
War Diary	Toupet	20/10/1918	20/10/1918
War Diary	Guignies	21/10/1918	26/10/1918
War Diary	Wez-Velvain	27/10/1918	31/10/1918
Heading	War Diary. of 15th Divisional Trench Mortar Brigade. (Volume 23) From 1st November 1918 To 30th November 1918		
War Diary	Velnain	01/11/1918	07/11/1918
War Diary	Bruyelle	08/11/1918	08/11/1918
War Diary	Antoing	09/11/1918	09/11/1918
War Diary	Baignies	10/11/1918	11/11/1918
War Diary	Moulbaix	12/11/1918	12/11/1918
War Diary	Chievres	13/11/1918	30/11/1918
Heading	War Diary of 15th Divisional Trench Mortar Brigade. (Volume 24) From 1st December 1918 To 31st December 1918		

War Diary	Chievres	01/12/1918	10/12/1918
War Diary	Moulbaix	11/12/1918	15/12/1918
War Diary	Tongre Notre Dame	16/12/1918	16/12/1918
War Diary	Horrues	17/12/1918	17/12/1918
War Diary	Rebecq	18/12/1918	31/12/1918
War Diary	War Diary. of 15th Divisional Trench Mortar Brigade. (Volume 25.) From 1st January 1919 To 31st January 1919		
War Diary	Rebecq-Rognon	01/01/1919	31/01/1919
Heading	War Diary of 15th Divisional Trench Mortar Brigade. (Volume 26) From 1st February 1919. To 28th February 1919		
War Diary	Rebecq Rognon	01/02/1919	08/02/1919

W655M / 19243(3)

W655M / 19243(3)

15TH DIVISION

15TH DIVL TRENCH MORTAR BTY.

AUG 1916 - MAR 1919

Confidential

War Diary
of
1st Div" Medium T.M. Batteries.
1-7-16 To 31-7-16

Army Form C. 2118

WAR DIARY July 1916 1st Divisional
or Trench Mortars
INTELLIGENCE SUMMARY
(Erase heading not required.)

Place	Date	Hour	Summary of Events and Information	Remarks and references to Appendices
Hohenzollern	July 1st		Guns placed in position in Highland Trench for wire cutting.	
Hulluch & Plouvain	2		Drills in conjunction with Infantry unit Rifle Grenade Shot.	
	3		Wire Cutting during the day about H.13.B.3-4 and H.13.B.5-5 in preparation to 10/11 H.L.I. bombing raid on night of 5th.	
	4			
	5			
	6		Wire Cutting about Bogas 115 & 117	
	7		Retaliation to Swan Mortars	
	8		On few damages and bombs	
	9		Trench Mortar Shot on same day and retaliation to Enemy mortar	
	10			
	11			
	12		Have Cutting along whole front at intervals during that day. Also retaliation	
	13		to Enemy Mortars.	
	14			
	15		Wire Cutting H.Ba.1/2-9/a to H.7.C.1-2/a in preparation for raid - was	
	16		Cutting also continued at various points along his	
	20		Proposed raid off - Information received that Division is to be relieved	
	23		Relief in Hulluch & Quarre sectors completed on the night - Battery return	
	29/30		to XI RAFA at Bully-la-Bourse.	

WAR DIARY July 1916.
or INTELLIGENCE SUMMARY
(Erase heading not required.)

Army Form C. 2118

1st Divisional Medium Trench Mortars

Place	Date	Hour	Summary of Events and Information	Remarks and references to Appendices
	23rd/24th		Battery in Hohenzollern Sector relieved on the right and return to Billets at Vermelles & South La Bourse.	
Monchy Breton	24th	At 2.30	Battery proceeds by Motor Lorry to Monchy-Breton.	6 x 1
	25.		Nothing to report.	
	26.	Parades 5.45 am	Monch-Cauct and marches to Vacquerie	
Vacquerie	27.	Parade 9 am	Vacquerie and marches to Mezerolles	
Mezerolles	28.	Parade 9 am	Mezerolles and marches to Bois Bergues	
Bois Bergues	29.		Nothing to report.	
	30.		Inspection under Brigadier General Macnaughten A.D.O.	
Bourdon	31.	7 am	Motor transport to Bourdon.	

A C Gillette Capt
1st Div: T. M.

C O N F I D E N T I A L.

War Diary

of

15th Divnl Trench Mortars.

From 1st September, 1916 to 30th September, 1916.

Volume Number 3.

[signature]

Major, R.A.

Bde Major 15th Divisional Arty.

15th Divisional Artillery.

15th DIVISIONAL TRENCH MORTAR OFFICER

AUGUST 1 9 1 6

Mar 19

CONFIDENTIAL.

WAR DIARY.

of

15th Divnl Trench Mortars.

From 1st August, 1916   to   31st August, 1916.

VOLUME Number   7

E Boyce
Major, R.A.
Brigade Major R.A., 15th Divisional Artillery.

Vol II

WAR DIARY August 1916
1st Divisional Medium Army Form C. 2118
— Trench Mortars Vol 1

INTELLIGENCE SUMMARY
(Erase heading not required.)

Instructions regarding War Diaries and Intelligence Summaries are contained in F.S. Regs., Part II. and the Staff Manual respectively. Title Pages will be prepared in manuscript.

Place	Date	Hour	Summary of Events and Information	Remarks and references to Appendices
Bovelon	1st.		Nothing to report.	
Bavelincourt	2nd.		Proceeded from Bovelon to Bavelincourt by Motor Lorry.	
	3rd.		Nothing to report.	
	4th.		Left Bavelincourt for Albert and proceeded to take our two guns in the line from 13th Division – from old of Action await to reach advance. Gun NCO + one OR. wounded against relief.	
Albert	5th.		Own offices + 5A OR. proceeded to 3rd Section 1st DAC. to whom they were attd. to loading + unloading Ammunition.	
	6th.		Battery Engages in building forward Shelters. Exchange to 1st DA filing up Shell hole + Enemies repairing roads to Divisional Artillery Battery Position and keeping roads in repair.	
	7th.		Gun places in position in High Wood in preparation for attack by 1st Division.	
	8th.	2.15 am	Enemy bombd + damages but in action again by 9.30 pm.	
	9th.		Battalion attacks to 3rd Sec. 1st DAC as before also in Shell hole and Road Repairing Fatigues.	
	10th to 27th.		At request of Infantry guns in High Wood Silenced Enemy Rifle grenades	
	28.			

Army Form C. 2118

WAR DIARY August 1916 1st Divisional Medium Trench Mortars
or
INTELLIGENCE SUMMARY

(Erase heading not required.)

Place	Date	Hour	Summary of Events and Information	Remarks and references to Appendices
	28th		Gun in High Wood taken over by 1st Division.	
	29 to 31.		Batteries attached to 3rd Sec. 1st D.A.C. for fatigue as before -	

A C Albert Capt
1st Div. T.M.O

Army Form C. 2118

X.Y.Z Trench Mortar Batteries — **WAR DIARY** September 1916

or

INTELLIGENCE SUMMARY

(Erase heading not required.)

Instructions regarding War Diaries and Intelligence Summaries are contained in F.S. Regs., Part II. and the Staff Manual respectively. Title Pages will be prepared in manuscript.

Y.2

Place	Date	Hour	Summary of Events and Information	Remarks and references to Appendices
	1/9		The 3 Batteries continued to supply the bulk of their personnel for duty with No 3 Section D.A.C. on Ammunition Supply (Order 50/554 22/8/16) up to 19th Division	
	6/10		1 Officer & 20 men relieved 3-18pr Guns (73 Brigade) { 2 nr Caterpillar Wood } { 1 Cotton Bayonet & Petit Wood }	
			2 Mortars were put into Clarke Trench & Bethel Sap under 1 Officer (Conroy) from Relieved by 50 Division	
	10		1 Mortar was taken over from 50 Div in Shelbourne Alley	
	11/20		2 further Mortars were put in on Divisional front, came into action on 15th & were handed over on 20th to the 23rd Div.	
	20		All 3 Batteries proceeded to St Graten & arrived late afternoon & evening	
	21/30		Supplied daily between 40 & 50 men to R.E. for filling & repairing screens	
	25/6		3 Officers & 3 RSOs attended instruction & practice with gas helmets at Montigny	

J H Garrett K.
for H.Y. M.O. XV Div—
2/10/16

C O N F I D E N T I A L.

War Diary

of

15th Divl Trench Mortars

1st October, 1916.   to   31st October, 1916.

VOLUME. 4.

E B Boyce

Major R.A.
Brigade Major 15th Divisional Arty.

vol 3

Army Form C. 2118.

WAR DIARY
or
INTELLIGENCE SUMMARY.
(Erase heading not required.)

Place	Date	Hour	Summary of Events and Information	Remarks and references to Appendices
	October			
Pt. GRATIEN	1		Divisional Rest – Battery proceed employed in getting passes.	
Pt. GRATIEN	2–5			
	6	3.pm	Battery proceeded by Motor lorry to Bécourt Wood – Relieved 23rd Division.	
O.G.I. East of Le Sars	9		4 guns taken out of line from 23rd Division – No guns in action.	
	10			
	11		1. Gun in action about M.16.c.	
	12		9th Division attack on Butte de WARLENCOURT – Attack failed to reach objectives – Mortars in Action.	
	13		1. Gun in action about M.15.B.2.9.	
	14			
	to		Firing done by both guns – Situation Quiet.	
	20			
	21		Canadian attack on W. of Le SARS. – Successful	
	22			
	23		Nothing to report.	

Army Form C. 2118.

WAR DIARY

INTELLIGENCE SUMMARY.

(Erase heading not required.)

Instructions regarding War Diaries and Intelligence Summaries are contained in F. S. Regs., Part II. and the Staff Manual respectively. Title pages will be prepared in manuscript.

Place	Date	Hour	Summary of Events and Information	Remarks and references to Appendices
	24		Guns moved forward to attack on 25th — In action.	
	25		Attack postponed	
	26		Nothing to report.	
	27			
	28		Attack postponed until 1st Nov.	
	29		Nothing to report.	
	30			
	31			

W. Stewart Capt.
P.T.T.O.
XI.

Army Form C. 2118.

WAR DIARY
or
INTELLIGENCE SUMMARY.
(Erase heading not required.)

Instructions regarding War Diaries and Intelligence Summaries are contained in F. S. Regs., Part II. and the Staff Manual respectively. Title pages will be prepared in manuscript.

Place	Date	Hour	Summary of Events and Information	Remarks and references to Appendices

1577 Wt.W10791/1773 500,000 1/15 D. D. & L. A.D.S.S./Forms/C. 2118.

CONFIDENTIAL.

War Diary.

of

15th Div T. m.Rly.

From 1st November, 1916 - 30th November, 1916.

VOLUME 5

1.11.16.

[signature] Captain,

for Bd Major 15th Divisional Arty.

Army Form C. 2118

WAR DIARY
or
INTELLIGENCE SUMMARY

1st Division Trench Mortars

Vol 4

(Erase heading not required.)

Place	Date	Hour	Summary of Events and Information	Remarks and references to Appendices
La SARS.	1st to 8th		No 2" Trench Mortars in action at Le Sars at M.16.D.4.8 Personnel of one Battery attached to 1st D.A.C. at M.25.D.	
	2nd & 3rd 4th		1st Division relieved by 48th Division	
Bécourt	8th		Relieved by 1st Division Trench Mortars – These Batteries proceed to rest at M.25.D and attached to 1st D.A.C.	
Bécourt	10th to 30th		Employed on the Construction of Horse Standings at X.15.C.d.	

A.C. Slade Capt
For Div T M O

CONFIDENTIAL

WAR DIARY

of

15th Divisional Trench Mortar Batteries

From 1st December, 1916 to 31st December, 1916.

VOLUME 6

Major, R.A.
Brigade Major 15th Divisional Artillery.

Army Form C. 2118.

WAR DIARY
or
INTELLIGENCE SUMMARY.
(Erase heading not required.)

1st Division Headquarters Branch Motors. Vol 5

Place	Date	Hour	Summary of Events and Information	Remarks and references to Appendices
BECOURT	1st	–	Nothing to report.	
"	to 31st		No Guns in Action during this period.	

A. Elliott Capt.
Xn Div. T.M.O.

Army Form C. 2118.

WAR DIARY
or
INTELLIGENCE SUMMARY.
(Erase heading not required.)

Instructions regarding War Diaries and Intelligence Summaries are contained in F. S. Regs., Part II. and the Staff Manual respectively. Title pages will be prepared in manuscript.

Place	Date	Hour	Summary of Events and Information	Remarks and references to Appendices

157 Wt.W10791/1773 500,000 1/15 D. D. & L. A.D.S.S./Forms/C. 2118.

Army Form C. 2118.

WAR DIARY
or
INTELLIGENCE SUMMARY.
(Erase heading not required.)

Instructions regarding War Diaries and Intelligence Summaries are contained in F.S. Regs., Part II. and the Staff Manual respectively. Title pages will be prepared in manuscript.

MEDIUM & HEAVY TRENCH MORTARS 15th DIVISION

Vol 6

Place	Date	Hour	Summary of Events and Information	Remarks and references to Appendices
BECOURT L. SARS.	1-3		3 Batter. of Fatigue building House Standings for 15th D.A.	
	5		1 2" T.M. placed in Action at M7c 2-5	
	6,7		Bombs Carried up and Dug out & Bomb Store commenced.	
	7½			
	8,11		Dug out & Bomb Store continued and Completed on 11th	
	12		1 2" T.M. placed in Action at M7c12-6½	
	14		Guns at M7c 2-5 reported on Butte, Butte Wich. 6 rounds fires at Butte & Butte Tr	
	15		do ½-6½ reported on Quarry at M7 A 0-6	
	16		Emplacement Commenced on Chalk Pit at M15 B 1-8	
	17		Emplacement Continued + Completed at M15 B 1-8	
	19		50 Bombs Carried to Guns at M7c 2-5.	
	20		50 do to do M15 B 1-8. — Heavy T.M.N⁵ formed at LAVIEVILLE	
Peake Wood	21		Heavy Battr. moved to Peake Wood. —	
	22		50 Bombs to Guns at M7c 2-5". — Heavy T.M. Emplacement Commenced at M16c 2½ 5½	
	23		150 2" Bombs to MARTINPUICH — Heavy T.M. Emplacement Continued	
	24		Heavy T.M. Emplacement Continued — Dug out & Bomb Store commenced in Chalk Pit for 2" MoA	
	25		Heavy T.M. do to do Continued	

A.C. Elliott Capt.
W.D.T.M.O.

Army Form C. 2118.

WAR DIARY
or
INTELLIGENCE SUMMARY.
(Erase heading not required.)

MEDIUM & HEAVY TRENCH MORTARS
5th DIVISION

Place	Date	Hour	Summary of Events and Information	Remarks and references to Appendices
Le SARS	CONTINUED			
	26.27.		Heavy T.M. Emplacement Continued – 2" T.M. Dug out & Bomb Store – Chalk Pit completed on 27 – 3 Bomb firs at Butte & Bull TR at Eaucourt working party.	
	28.		Mortar at Mine 2-5 moved to Mine 2-14 to fire at M.16.B.8-5½ – M.16.38-8. – no reports – and 5 rounds fired – took cover in African T.M. Emplacement.	
	29/30	1:45am	Raid by 44th Infantry Brigade on Butte de Warlencourt – Successful – 38 Bombs fired by 2" Trench Mortars – work continued on Heavy T.M. Emplacement at Le Sars. 30 ft of Tunneling completed to date also Ammunition used to hold 50 rounds of 9.45" Ammunition – work being continued.	

1.2.17

A.C. Elliott Capt
5th Div T.M.O

CONFIDENTIAL

WAR DIARY

OF

15th. DIVISIONAL TRENCH MORTAR BATTERIES.

FOR MONTH OF FEBRUARY 1917.

VOLUME XX

E. Boyce
Maj RA.
for Brig:General.
Commanding 15th.Divisional Artillery.

Army Form C. 2118

WAR DIARY
or
INTELLIGENCE SUMMARY
(Erase heading not required.)

Instructions regarding War Diaries and Intelligence Summaries are contained in F.S. Regs., Part II. and the Staff Manual respectively. Title Pages will be prepared in manuscript.

Vol 7

Place	Date	Hour	Summary of Events and Information	Remarks and references to Appendices
	1917 Feb 1/4		2 2" Guns in Right Sector Hecham Rd.	
	5		1.2. left a Chalk Pit	
			Entraining emplacement & tunnelling for 1. 9.45" Gun in Left Sector	
	1/10		Handed over to 2nd Australian Div"	
	6		Y/15 Battery attended IV Army T.M. School at Vaux-en-Amienois	
	10		X, Z, V Batteries left Becourt & Peake Wood respectively & proceeded to Laviéville	
	11		Y do proceeded from Vaux to Laviéville	
	5		All Batteries at Laviéville. The training of 35 Gun r Div D.A.C. personnel commenced	
	16		All Batteries marched from Laviéville to Hem	
	17		D. Hem to Monchy	
	18		D. Monchy to Roellencourt	
	19		Training of D.A.C. personnel continued at Roellencourt	
	25		All Batteries (minus 2 Off. & 12 O.R. left for training purposes) proceeded from Roellencourt &	
	26		took up pos" in Arras	
	27		Took over (1.3 Sects VI Corps) G.30.a 65.85 to the R. Scarpe.	

W.A. Gowith Lt. Col.
Actg XV ITMO
1/3/17

CONFIDENTIAL

War Diary

of

15th Div. T.M.

From 1st March 1917   -   To 31st March 1917

Volume IX

Army Form C. 2118

WAR DIARY or INTELLIGENCE SUMMARY
(Erase heading not required.)

Place	Date	Hour	Summary of Events and Information	Remarks and references to Appendices
Arras	1917 1/31 March		Operations: Cutting of enemy wire (mainly front line) which was successful. Preparation of 3 - 9.45" 14 - 2" mortars } Bombardment along Completion of 5 - 6 - } Division front Q.30b 1.8 to R.Scarpe. Training of reinforcements prior to course at III Army School was continued. Eng detach { 1 Off & 6 OR each. Heavy & Medium Batteries at { Roclincourt 1/10 March Harbarcq 12/9 — Officers & men trained at III Army School	Vol 9

	9.45" Gun				2" Gun			
	Gunners		Infantry		Gunners		Infantry	
	Off	OR	Off	OR	Off	OR	Off	OR
Bacre 2/9		8						
Do. 11/19	1	25	2	33	3	35	3	35
Do. 2/30					8	1	7	
	1	33	2	33	3	43	4	42

WAR DIARY
or
INTELLIGENCE SUMMARY
(Erase heading not required.)

Army Form C. 2118

Place	Date	Hour	Summary of Events and Information	Remarks and references to Appendices
	1917			
	1/31 March		Mentioned Anti Gas Course Aberdaught 13/16 March 92621 Cpl W. Morris V/15 Battery	
			28/31 — 9620 — T. Duncan " "	
			Quarters in Arras :— Mess Billets { 20, 26, 70 } Rue St. Maurice H.Qrs 3 Place Victor Hugo	
			Casualties resulting from enemy fire { Killed S. Wounded Wounded Slight	
			13 OR 2 OR 1 Off 2 OR 1 Off 3 OR	
	23 March		Casualties in action (premature) 2 OR.	
	29	5a.m.	Enemy shell caused explosion of our 300 rds 9.45" Amn at Store G.23.d.8.2.8½. & resulted in casualties V/15 Battery (13 OR Killed 10 OR wounded) included above	
			also some casualties among the Scottish Rifles	
			Ammunition expended 2,474 rds 2" 185 rds 9.45"	

H.D. Garrett L.
Capt/Adjt. L TMB

CONFIDENTIAL.

War Diary

of

15th D.T.M.

VOLUME 4

From 1st April 1917 . 30th April, 1917.

Army Form C. 2118.

WAR DIARY
or
INTELLIGENCE SUMMARY.
(Erase heading not required.)

Place	Date	Hour	Summary of Events and Information	Remarks and references to Appendices
	APRIL 1		Medium Batteries fired 152 rounds at targets on enemy's 1st & 2nd line system. Fairly good results. Several B.A.P.O's began to open out. 14 Rounds 9.45" at enemy emplacements. One explosion caused and much debris thrown up.	
	2		176 Rounds 2" fired on front and support wires. Some damage caused but high wind made accurate shooting difficult. 33 Rounds 9.45" fired at houses in BLANGY and at gun emplacements. 3 houses received direct hits and timber from emplacements was removed.	
	3		Enemy observed to have repairs wire. Several B.A.P.O's on ist line & support wire. Several pfc rounds in enemy front trench, dull thuds & stinkers dislodged. Effect on 1st support wire not observed, but enemy retaliated vigorously. Fritz considerably increased his S.A.A. fire. 209 rounds 2" fired concentrated on strong points, dugouts, front line trench. 9.45" a.a. gun bombarded houses and emplacements at BLANGY, numerous direct hits obtained and much masonry & timber thrown up.	
	4		575 Rounds 2" fired at enemy wire system and sap heads, good results on wire & quantity stakes demolished. Heavy enemy retaliation. 2 guns twice endeavour to dig out. Thrown in. Heavies opened fire with full battery. 100 Rounds fired on strong points, dugouts, front line trench, sunken roads and salient. Shooting very effective.	
	5		457 Rounds 2" fired on front line & support wire about sap heads. Great damage caused. (Premature) in No1 gun caused 3 faulty guns. 1 Bombardier killed. Same targets engaged by Heavy Battery, as in the 4th. 109 rounds 9.5" fired. Good results obtained and quantity timber thrown up along railway.	
	6		Night firing carried out by all Batteries. 438 Rounds 2" fired. Much wire removed & M.S. position blown up. Considerable enemy retaliation. 9 & 7 gun emplacements blown in and much ammunition burst. Right section of the Ly Battery bombarded enemy support line & left section front line. 100 Rounds fired	
	7		2" TM fire concentrates on enemy wire and sap heads. 560 rounds fired wire practically flat. 100 Rounds 9.45" fired on front & support lines. Much debris thrown up. All battery concentrates on enemy works 6am 657 rounds 2" fired. Considerable damage caused. 120 Rounds 45" fired Several houses at BLANGY (containing machine guns) clean light. Quantity of S.A.A. ammunition destroyed during night by enemy retaliation.	
	8-9			

Army Form C. 2118.

WAR DIARY
or
INTELLIGENCE SUMMARY.
(Erase heading not required.)

Place	Date	Hour	Summary of Events and Information	Remarks and references to Appendices
	10.		15 Casualties to personnel between April 1 - 9.	
			Assisted D.A.C. on ammunition dump.	
	11		Infantry personnel, attached to 5 fort attack, rejoined respective units.	
			Guns removed from line, also cleaned and prepared for future exigencies.	
			Gun stores checked.	
	11-30		5 - 2" guns damaged in actions sent to Ordnance for necessary attention.	
			Assisted D.A.C. at ammunition dumps.	
			Supplied fatigue parties for D.A. Signals.	
			Number of captured guns asked and conveyed to Ordnance.	
			French Mortar Ammunition collected.	

O.S. Winterton
Lt D.T.M.O.

CONFIDENTIAL.

WAR DIARY

of

15th DIVISIONAL TRENCH MORTAR BATTERIES.

from 1st May, 1917. to 31st May, 1917.

(Volume 5).

Army Form C. 2118.

WAR DIARY
INTELLIGENCE SUMMARY. 15th T.M.n Trench Mortar Bty.
(Erase heading not required.)

Instructions regarding War Diaries and Intelligence Summaries are contained in F. S. Regs., Part II. and the Staff Manual respectively. Title pages will be prepared in manuscript.

Place	Date	Hour	Summary of Events and Information	Remarks and references to Appendices
In the field	1.5.17 to 23.5.17		Fatigue Work. — Collecting & scavenging Trench Mortar Bombs. D.A. Signals fatigues. Camouflage collecting. Field Artillery Brigade fatigues. Divisional Ammunition Dump fatigues. Corps H.A. Ammunition Dump fatigues. Cleaning Trench Mortar Guns. From "Action" to "Rest" position.	No XI
	24.5.17 to 26.5.17		Line of March. —	
	27.5.17 to 31.5.17		Physical Exercises & Gun Drill. Recreation & Training for Divisional Sports. Musketry Practice.	

A Gibb. Capt.
XV.DT.M.O.

A5834. Wt.W4973/M687 750,000 8/16 D.D.&L.Ltd. Forms/C.2118/13

CONFIDENTIAL.

WAR DIARY

of

15th DIVISIONAL TRENCH MORTAR BATTERIES.

From 1st June, 1917.   To 30th June 1917.

VOLUME 6.

WAR DIARY
for June 1917
INTELLIGENCE SUMMARY

Army Form C. 2118.

Vol 12

15th Divisional Trench Mortar Bys

Place	Date	Hour	Summary of Events and Information	Remarks and references to Appendices
MONCHEL	1-6-17 / 15-6-17		In rest billets at MONCHEL. Training. Party of 30 HAC personnel given instruction on T.M's	
MONCHEL	16-6-17	3 a.m.	Assisting French farmers. Leaving – Marched to new billets at TENEUR	
TENEUR	17-6-17	3 a.m.	Marched to new billets at FONTES	
FONTES	18-6-17	3 a.m.	Marched to new billets at STEENBECQUE	
STEENBECQUE	19-6-17		Batteries remained at billets in STEENBECQUE for the day	
STEENBECQUE	20-6-17	11 a.m.	Marched to new billets 2 kilos E of STEENVOORDE	
STEENVOORDE	21-6-17	10 a.m.	Advance Party marched to WATOU. drew tents from 2nd Aus Commandants & pitched camp S. of WATOU	
			Batteries marched to WATOU at camp	
WATOU	22-6-17	9:15 p.m.	Cleaned 2" guns.	
WATOU	23-6-17		Checked gun stores	
WATOU	24-6-17	10 a.m.	Advance Party left WATOU for VLAMERTINGHE where Headquarters of T.M. are situated	
YPRES	24-6-17		Daily Tash over by Heavy T.M positions and Medium T.M positions on the line	
WATOU	25-6-17		Lectures by officers on defensive measures against enemy gas.	
WATOU	26-6-17		Lectures by officers on trench warfare as adapted to Trench Mortars	
WATOU	27-6-17	11 p.m.	Cleaned guns.	
WATOU	28-6-17	10 p.m.	Batteries proceeded to new Trench Mortar Headquarters at VLAMERTINGHE	
VLAMERTINGHE	29-6-17		Transported guns and ammunition to positions in line	
VLAMERTINGHE	30-6-17	9 a.m.	5" C.R. proceeded to VII Army School of Mortars for instruction on the 6" NEWTON TRENCH MORTAR.	

O. C. Kirk Capt.
VI. T.M.B.
27/7/18

CONFIDENTIAL.

WAR DIARY

of

15th Divisional Trench Mortar Batteries

(Volume 7)

From 1st July 1917. To 31st July 1917.

WAR DIARY of 15th Div.¹ Trench Mortar Btys
INTELLIGENCE SUMMARY. (JULY)

Vol / 3

Army Form C. 2118.

Place	Date 1917 July	Hour	Summary of Events and Information	Remarks and references to Appendices
YPRES	1-4		Emplacements and Ammunition Recesses commenced in the line for the reception of 1, 2, 2-inch, 4-9.45-inch and 3-6-inch Newton Trench Mortars, Guns and Ammunition.	
	5&6		Work in line continued. Fatigue parties supplied to T.M.D.C. to clear and tidy up Dump.	
	7		Work in line continued. Received 3.6-inch Newton Trenches 2 Nos.	
	8		Bombs conveyed to line.	
	9		200 Bombs carried to disused trench stables.	
	10		Work on positions in line continued. 200 Bombs carried to positions.	
	10		2-9.45-inch Trench Mortars received.	
	11		1-9.45 mgf Trench Mortar together with Ammunition and Component Parts conveyed to line. 250 bombs carried to positions	
	12		280-6" bombs conveyed to line.	
	13		1-9.45-inch Trench Mortar conveyed to line, also beds & timber for emplacement.	
	14		300-6-inch bombs and 52-9.45-inch bombs conveyed to line.	
	15		Fatigue party supplied for strengthening O.Ps.	
	16		2-6-inch Newton guns taken to Champagne and 1-6-inch Newton received.	
			Positions in line completed ready for action.	
	17		23-2"inch fired at Mound. Effective shooting.	
	18		24-6-inch fired at Mound. Small auto made in wire.	
	19		43-2-inch and 25-6-inch fired. Wire damaged	
	19		45-2-inch fired. Gap made in wire of 10 yards	
	20		25-6-inch fired. 3 gaps of 5 to 7 yards.	
			19-2-inch and 21-6-inch fired. Much wire destroyed & gaps increased.	
			One position destroyed.	
	21		85-2-inch fired. Wire much damaged but observation over enemy reserve line difficult.	
			New positions commenced to replace the one destroyed on the 20th	
	22		83-2-inch fired. Good wire thrown up.	
			40-9.45-inch fired. Enemy dump struck and blown up.	
			67-6-inch fired on enemy's reserve line.	
			71-2-inch fired. Gaps enlarged & increased.	
	23		25-9.45-inch fired. Quantity debris unearthed thrown up to the air.	
			New position commenced on the 21st inst. completed and fired from.	
	24		118-2-inch, 38-9.45-inch and 47-6-inch fired in conjunction with raid made by the 12th H.L.I.	

(2)

WAR DIARY of 15th Div.l Trench Mortar Btys Army Form C. 2118.

INTELLIGENCE SUMMARY. (JULY)

(Erase heading not required)

Instructions regarding War Diaries and Intelligence Summaries are contained in F. S. Regs., Part II. and the Staff Manual respectively. Title pages will be prepared in manuscript.

Place	1917 Date July	Hour	Summary of Events and Information	Remarks and references to Appendices
YPRES	25		8 5"-2 inch fired. Quantity of wire flattened and dump exploded in enemy's lines. 3 5"-9"45inch fired. Gaps extended and wire further damaged. 2 3"-6 inch fired. Emplacements on enemy's emplacements.	
	26		7 3"-2 inch fired. Gaps greatly increased. 1 1"-9"45 inch fired. Full details removed. 4 1"-6 inch fired. Effective shooting on to enemy positions	
	27		2 5"-6 inch fired. Explosion caused in enemy's line. 2 7"-9"45inch fired. Enemy gas cylinders believed to have been hit. Smoke observed drifting over enemy trenches. 8 9"-2 inch fired - Gaps further increased.	
	28		5 4"-2 inch and 2 5"-6 inch fired in support of raid.	
	29		7 3"-2 inch and 2 2"-6 inch fired. Great quantity of wire removed. 2 0"-9"45 inch fired at all points on enemy line.	
	30		11 7"-2 inch fired at support line. 12 6"-6 inch fired at enemy trench Mortar emplacement. 1 1"-9"45 inch fired at enemy trench Mortar emplacement.	
	31		Firing continued to ZERO hour. Two fatigue parties of 50 men each under officers supplied at ZERO hour. No. 3 Track repaired and pushing forward condition in one party and assistance given in clearing up the old battery positions vacated by the 70th Brigade R.F.A. by the other party.	

a.c.ruir. Capt.
15th Divisional Trench Mortar Officer.

CONFIDENTIAL.

WAR DIARY

of

15th Divisional Trench Mortar Batteries.

From 1st August 1917. To 31st August 1917.

(Volume 8.)

Army Form C. 2118.

Vol 14
15th Divisional Trench Mortar Btys

WAR DIARY
INTELLIGENCE SUMMARY.
(Erase heading not required.)

Instructions regarding War Diaries and Intelligence Summaries are contained in F. S. Regs., Part II. and the Staff Manual respectively. Title pages will be prepared in manuscript.

Place	Date 1917 August	Hour	Summary of Events and Information	Remarks and references to Appendices
YPRES.	1-6		Staking enemy Trench Mortars and conveying same to billets	
	7-9		Cleaning and painting salved Trench Mortars	
	10-20		Ammunition fatigues Ammunition fatigues at D.A.C. dump. Ammunition fatigues at Brigade Wagon Lines.	
	21-22		fatigues at D.A.H.Q.	
	23		fatigues for D.A.H.Q.	
	24		Cable burying fatigues in trenches.	
	25		Ammunition fatigues	
	26		1.6" NEWTON Trench Mortars conveyed to line	
	27		1-9·45" Trench Mortars conveyed to line and put in on FREZENBERG the RIDGE.	
	28		1-9·45" Trench Mortars conveyed to line and put in GREY RUINS	
			1-9·45" fired at BORRY FARM.	
			1-9·45" fired at BECK HOUSE & BORRY FARM.	
	29-31		2-9·45" fired at BORRY FARM and BECK HOUSE	

A Elliott Capt
15th D.T.M.O.

CONFIDENTIAL.

WAR DIARY

Of

15th Divisional Trench Mortar Batteries.

(Volume 9).

From 1/9/17.

To 30/9/17.

Army Form C. 2118.

WAR DIARY
of
INTELLIGENCE SUMMARY.
15th Div[isiona]l Trench Mortar Batteries.
(Erase heading not required.)

Vol 15

Instructions regarding War Diaries and Intelligence Summaries are contained in F. S. Regs., Part II. and the Staff Manual respectively. Title pages will be prepared in manuscript.

Place	1917 Date Sept	Hour	Summary of Events and Information	Remarks and references to Appendices
WATOU	1		Batteries resting preparatory to moving.	
NOORDPEENE	2-3		V/15 Trench Mortar Battery marched to NOORDPEENE	
WORMHOUDT	2-3		X, Y, Z/15 Trench Mortar Batteries marched to WORMHOUDT	
	4		Batteries on fatigue duties at CASSEL and WORMHOUDT stations respectively for loading trucks for F.A.Y.	
CASSEL WORMHOUDT	5		Batteries entrained for ARRAS. Marched to HABARCQ from ARRAS STATION.	
HABARCQ FAMPOUX ATHIES	6-7		Awaiting orders to proceed to line and take over.	
	8		V/15 French Mortar B[atter]y relieved V/4 Trench Mortar B[atter]y — 1.9.45 in action.	
	9		X, Y/15 French Mortar B[atter]ys relieved X, Y, Z/4 Trench Mortar B[atter]ys — 3-2" T.M/s in action.	
	10-30		Working parties in line constructing emplacements & ammunition recesses for guns, and dug outs for detachments. Preparing kit etc. for gunless quarters.	
	14		20 rounds 9.45" fired at enemy's emplacement, causing considerable damage. Mg's &.b. Mount & another damaged. Two Germans seen leaving emplacement wt sniped.	
	15		17 rounds 2" T.M's put in action	
	16		2 - 2" T.M's fired in conjunction with raid.	
	17		2 - 2" T.M's put in action	
	18		19 rounds 9.45" fired. Enemy trench considerably damaged.	
	19		17 rounds 9.45" fired at enemies emplacement and dugout. 1 top.b damaged and much trench thrown up.	
	20		1 - 2" T.M in action	
	21		35 - 2" fired at enemywire. 9 direct hits in wire and 6 on enemy front line. Gaps off from 20 yds. to 5 yds.	
	22		1 - 9" T.M put in action.	
	23		40 rounds 2" fired. Wire and Stokes Mortar ayd. Series of small explosions caused by one round	
	24		70 rounds 2" fired. Grenade dump. Gap about 25 yds made.	
			29 rounds 2" fired. 2 gaps about 15 yds. made. Large explosion caused probably small Am[munitio]n. dad on T.M. store.	
	25		19 rounds 9.45 fired at dugouts. One badly damaged	
			15 rounds 2" wire considerably damaged. 1 explosion caused.	
			16 rounds 2" at selected targets. Effective shooting.	
	26		15 - 9.45 fired at camouflaged shell-holes and in searching recently	
	27		29 rounds 2" fired. Wire and Stokes Thrower ayd, and much debris. VERY LIGHT dumps set on fire —	
	28		3/3 rounds 2" fired at wire and hostile MINENWERFER position. Latter effectively silenced. Shayraph' effect off.	
	29		3.2 rounds 2" fired at wire and debris thrown up. No 3 emplacement damaged for a bay b 10 yd. Quantity of wood wire and debris thrown up. Caps of about 10 yd's made wire and stakes blown up.	
	30		4.5 rounds 2" fired at enemy wire. Caps of about 10 yd made wire and stakes blown up.	

A.B.White Capt
15th D.T.M.B.

CONFIDENTIAL.

WAR DIARY

of

15th Divisional Trench Mortar Batteries.

From 1st October 1917. To 31st October, 1917.
(Volume 10).

Army Form C. 2118.

No.

WAR DIARY
for October 1917
INTELLIGENCE SUMMARY: 15th Divisional Trench Mortar Batteries
(Erase heading not required.)

Place	Date October	Hour	Summary of Events and Information	Remarks and references to Appendices
ROEUX and MONCHY	1		15 rounds 9·45" fired at camouflaged shell holes. 6 shuns observed to give same 37 rounds 2" fired at enemy wire system. Wood and debris thrown up	
	2		28 rounds 2" fired. Explosion caused in enemy lines.	
	3		17 rounds 9·45" fired at enemy emplacement. Considerable damage caused. 33 rounds 2" fired. All effective. One dump, probably S.A.A. fuel, exp in support DEVILS TRENCH	
	4		41 rounds 2" fired. Much wire thrown up. Two of these rounds fired at night during enemy S.O.S.	
	5		49 rounds 2" fired. Number of posts blown into air and one gap noticed by about 5 yards.	
	6		48 rounds 2" fired. Some of these at enemy front line. Debris was thrown up. 21 rounds 9·45" fired at M.G. emplacement and dug-outs. 17 rounds 2" fired. Majority of these were fired during raid, at allotted targets 14 rounds 6" fired during raid.	
	7		31 rounds 2" fired. Gaps enlarged and wire further damaged. Enemy wiring partly disrupted.	
	8		6 rounds 6" fired in retaliation to enemy mortar.	
	9		11 rounds 2" fired. Observation difficult. Work on emplacement prevented further firing 10 rounds 6" fired at CHALK PIT.	
	10		9 rounds 9·45" fired at CHALK PIT. 33 rounds 2" fired. Wire further damaged. Gap at one point increased. 20 rounds 6" fired at T.M. and M.G. emplacements.	
	11		38 rounds 2" fired. Gaps of about 10 yards and 8 yards now visible. Further gap increased. 9 rounds 9·45" fired at T.M. emplacement. Observation difficult owing to low visibility.	
	12		49 rounds 2" fired. Gap at one point about 30 to 40 yards. Other damage could not be observed.	

Army Form C. 2118.

WAR DIARY
for October 1917
INTELLIGENCE SUMMARY.
(Erase heading not required.)

No. 2.

15th Divisional Trench Mortar Batteries

Place: ROEUX and MONCHY

Date October	Hour	Summary of Events and Information	Remarks and references to Appendices
13		53 rounds 2" fired. Direct hits obtained on wire and gaps increased. 3 rounds 6" fired in retaliation to enemy T.M. in CHALK PIT.	
14		13 rounds 9.45 fired at occupied houses. Considerable damage to masonry. 60 rounds 2" fired. Gaps in wire increased and points repaired by enemy again restored.	
15		32 rounds 6" fired during raid by 61st and 12th Divisions. 20 rounds 9.45 fired. Direct hit obtained on hostile T.M. 42 rounds 2" fired. Further damage to wire and one fresh gap cut. 4 rounds 6" fired in retaliation to enemy T.M.	
16.		11 rounds 9.45 fired into PELVES. Several direct hits on houses. 44 rounds 2" fired. Quantity of wire thrown up.	
17.		22 rounds 6" fired. 16 rounds 9.45 at M.D. in PEARL TRENCH. 3 rounds effective. 68 rounds 2" fired. About 20 yards wire cleared. 17 rounds 6" fired. 13 fell in wire.	
18		74 rounds 9.45 fired at occupied houses in PELVES and camouflaged shell holes. 8 rounds 2" fired. Stakes blown up and wire further damaged. 25 rounds 6" fired. Large gaps reported.	
19.		25 rounds 9.45 fired at CROSS ROADS. Large crater made in centre of road. Five S? Three rounds 6" fired in retaliation to hostile mortar. 66 rounds 2" fired. Several gaps made. 30 rounds 6" fired in retaliation to enemy T.M's in CHALK PIT. 20 rounds 9.45 fired into PELVES at occupied houses and into JUNCTION COPSE in retaliation.	
20.		53 rounds 2" fired. Several gaps now made from 10 to 20 yards in width. 80 rounds 6" fired at wire and in retaliation to hostile T.M. in CHALK PIT.	

Army Form C. 2118.

WAR DIARY

No 3.

for October 1917

INTELLIGENCE SUMMARY.

15th Divisional Trench Mortar Batteries

(Erase heading not required.)

Instructions regarding War Diaries and Intelligence Summaries are contained in F. S. Regs., Part II. and the Staff Manual respectively. Title pages will be prepared in manuscript.

Place: ROEUX and MONCHY

Date October	Hour	Summary of Events and Information	Remarks and references to Appendices
21		10 rounds 9.45" at HAUSA WOOD.	
		22 rounds 2" fired. Two fresh gaps made and enemy concertina wire cut.	
		31 rounds 6" fired. Two gaps of 15 and 10 yards respectively made.	
22		10 rounds 9.45" at SUNKEN ROAD. Three rounds effected Weithillypoor.	
		64 rounds 2" fired. Gaps increased and surrounding wire damaged.	
		26 rounds 6" at wire also at suspected T.M. in BARROT TRENCH	
23		20 rounds 9.45 at enemy trenches	
		88 rounds 2" fired with further damage to wire.	
24		15 rounds 9.45" at DELBAR WOOD. Twelve hits in wood.	
		49 rounds 2" fired - wire damaged but no increase in gaps reported.	
		30 rounds 6" fired. Gaps about 15 yards made.	
25		41 rounds 2" fired? Shooting very erratic owing to high wind.	
		10 rounds 6" fired?	
26 27		64 rounds 2" fired. Explosion caused in front line trench.	
		8 rounds 9.45 at occupied houses in PESVIS. Four fell in centre of village.	
		67 rounds 2" fired. Wire considerably damaged but no further gaps reported.	
		32 rounds 6" in reply to T.M's in CHARK PIT area.	
28		25 rounds 9.45" at M.G. emplacements and in retaliation to T.M's. Several good hits obtained	
		which dispersed enemy.	
		62 rounds 2" fired. Small gas about 5 yards. Enemy wiring party dispersed at 4.a.m.	
20		34 rounds 8" in retaliation to enemy mortars.	
29		9 rounds 9.45" at CHARK PIT. Ten T.M. round bursting muffled gun. 3-O.R. killed, 3-O.R. wounded.	
		61 rounds 2" fired - wire damaged - no further gaps	
		63 rounds 6" in retaliation to enemy mortars.	
30.		43 rounds 2" fired. One gap which has been repaired again cleared.	
		21 rounds 6" fired at wire and in retaliation to enemy T.M's.	

Army Form C. 2118.

WAR DIARY
for October 1917
INTELLIGENCE SUMMARY.
(Erase heading not required.)

No. 4

15th Divisional Trench Mortar Batteries

Place	Date October	Hour	Summary of Events and Information	Remarks and references to Appendices
ROEUX and MONCHY	31		10 rounds 9.45" at Cross Roads and trenches in vicinity. Direct hits obtained. 3 rounds 2" fired. One new gap reported. 57 rounds 6" at wire and in retaliation to enemy mortars	
	1-31		In addition to above, work was carried out during month, preparing dug outs and building emplacements for 6" N&M TOH T.M's.	

A.E. Rusk Capt.
15th D.T.M.O.

Army Form C. 2118.

WAR DIARY

15th Div" Trench Mortar Batteries
INTELLIGENCE SUMMARY. for NOVEMBER-1917.

(Erase heading not required.)

Instructions regarding War Diaries and Intelligence Summaries are contained in F. S. Regs., Part II. and the Staff Manual respectively. Title pages will be prepared in manuscript.

Place	Date November	Hour	Summary of Events and Information	Remarks and references to Appendices
ROEUX & MONCHY	1		10 rounds 9.45" fired at M.G. emplacement. Considerable damage caused.	
			30 rounds 2" fired. Gaps made and wire considerably damaged.	
			97 rounds 6" fired at wire, gaps in retaliation.	
	2		44 rounds 2" fired in retaliation.	
			31 rounds 6" fired. Two fresh gaps made in enemy wire.	
	3		4 rounds 9.45" fired at CROSS ROADS.	
			55 rounds 2" fired - wire further damaged.	
			46 rounds 6" fired. Gap slightly increased.	
	4		53 rounds 2" fired. Possibly hit.	
			84 rounds 6" in retaliation.	
	5		13 rounds 9.45" fired at CROSS ROADS - 6 direct hits on road.	
			41 rounds 2" fired - further damage to wire.	
			44 rounds 6" fired in retaliation.	
	6		35 rounds 2" fired. Gaps widened.	
			45 rounds 6" fired in retaliation.	
	7		57 rounds 2" fired. Gaps improved.	
			122 rounds 6" fired at wire and in retaliation to enemy T.M'S.	
	8		33 rounds 2" fired at allotted targets in support of raid.	
			147 rounds 6" fired 2nd gun fired in retaliation, 1st shelling day & night to prevent enemy repairing wire. Remainder fired during raid.	
	9		67 rounds 2" fired at wire and enemy saps. No increase in gaps.	
			37 rounds 6" fired in retaliation.	
	10		10 rounds 9.45" fired at RICE TRENCH - Six rounds effective in trench.	
			17 rounds 2" fired - wire damaged.	
			53 rounds 6" fired in retaliation to enemy T.M'S.	
	11		34 rounds 2" fired. Direct hits obtained on wire and further damage caused.	
			67 rounds 6" fired at enemy wire and in retaliation.	
	12		12 rounds 9.45" fired at APE TRENCH - 11 rounds effective.	
			33 rounds 2" fired. Wire considerably damaged.	
			44 rounds 6" fired in retaliation to enemy T.M'S.	

Army Form C. 2118.

WAR DIARY
15th Div: Trench Mortar Batteries
INTELLIGENCE SUMMARY. for NOVEMBER 1917.

(Erase heading not required.)

Instructions regarding War Diaries and Intelligence Summaries are contained in F. S. Regs., Part II. and the Staff Manual respectively. Title pages will be prepared in manuscript.

Place	Date NOVEMBER	Hour	Summary of Events and Information	Remarks and references to Appendices
ROEUX / MONCHY	13		12 rounds 9"+5" fired at CROSS RDS. Two direct hits obtained. MG emplacement suppressed.	
	14		29 rounds 2" fired. Wire considerably damaged. 87 rounds 6" fired.	
	15		12 rounds 9·45" fired at dugouts according to programme. 34 rounds 2" fired. 3 clear gaps of about 10 yds at each visible. 106 rounds 6" fired for registration and retaliation.	
	16		12 rounds 9·45" fired at M.G. and surrounding trenches. 9 direct hits obtained. 23 rounds 2" fired - gaps increased. 93 rounds 6" fired at wire and junction of POWDER F. DEV & 3 TRENCH. Several direct hits obtained.	
	17		7 rounds 9·45" at camouflaged shell holes. 10 rounds 2" fired at enemy wire. 153 rounds 6" fired at wire and in retaliation. Gap about 20 yards made.	
	18		14 rounds 2" fired. 369 rounds 6" fired at CROSS ROADS.	
	19		12 rounds 9·45" fired at CROSS ROADS. 5 rounds 2" fired during raid. 262 rounds 6" fired in conjunction with Artillery bombardment and during raid.	
	20		28 rounds 2" fired at enemy wire. 198 rounds 6" fired during raid and in retaliation. 4 rounds 9·45" fired at CROSS ROADS during raid.	
	21		26 rounds 2" fired at enemy wire. 177 rounds 6" fired in retaliation and in support of raid. 9·45" T.M. removed to fresh emplacement. 58 rounds 2" fired at enemy wire and in retaliation. 142 rounds 6" fired at junctions of enemy trenches, and in support of raid.	
	22		45 rounds 2" fired during enemy bombardment. 201 rounds 6" fired in accordance with Artillery programme and on S.O.S. lines during enemy bombardment.	

Army Form C. 2118.

WAR DIARY
15th Div: Trench Mortar Batteries
INTELLIGENCE SUMMARY. for NOVEMBER 1917.

(Erase heading not required.)

Instructions regarding War Diaries and Intelligence Summaries are contained in F. S. Regs., Part II. and the Staff Manual respectively. Title pages will be prepared in manuscript.

Place	Date NOVEMBER	Hour	Summary of Events and Information	Remarks and references to Appendices
ROEUX & MONCHY.	23		45 rounds 2" fired at enemy wire.	
	24		145 rounds 6" fired. Special trip wire which has been put out was well hit then.	
			19 rounds 2" fired. One 2" gun and ammunition buried.	
			144 rounds 6" fired at enemy wire and in retaliation.	
	25		10 rounds 2" fired - One gap of about 2 yds made.	
			137 rounds 6" fired. Two gaps 4 about 2 yds each made.	
	26		10 rounds 2" fired - Wire damaged.	
			160 rounds 6" fired. Wire badly damaged further gaps made.	
	27		58 rounds 6" fired at enemy mortars - Visibility poor. High wind prevents further firing.	
	28		8-9.45 "fired for registration.	
			35 rounds 6" fired in retaliation to enemy mortars -	
	29		49 rounds 6" fired in retaliation.	
	30		20 rounds 6" fired in retaliation.	

Louis Grey(?) Lt.
for Major
for. 15th D.T.M.B.

A.5834. Wt.W.4973/M687 750,000 8/16 D. D. & L. Ltd. Forms/C.2118/13

CONFIDENTIAL.

WAR DIARY

of

15th Divisional Trench Mortar Brigade

(Volume 12).

From 1st December 1917.　　　　　　　　to 31st December 1917.

Army Form C. 2118.

WAR DIARY
15th D.I.V. Trench M/8/8 by Bde No. I
INTELLIGENCE SUMMARY.
for December 1917.

VII 18

Instructions regarding War Diaries and Intelligence Summaries are contained in F. S. Regs. Part II and the Staff Manual respectively. Title pages will be prepared in manuscript.

Place	Date 1917	Hour	Summary of Events and Information	Remarks and references to Appendices
ROEUX	1		19 rounds 6" fired at wire and in retaliation	
	2		No firing reports	
	3		83 rounds 6" fired in retaliation — some Very lights	
			18 rounds 9.45" fired at APE TRENCH. Very lights & wind	
	4		39 rounds 6" fired in retaliation to hostile T.M's.	
	5		9 rounds 6" fired at CORN TRENCH.	
	6		11 rounds 9.45" fired at hostile T.M. and in response to S.O.S.	
	7		30 rounds 6" fired at CARROT & CARAVAN TRENCHES	
			40 rounds 6" fired at enemy working parties abouts fire returned	
	8		9 rounds 9.45" fired at enemy M.G. emplacements. Good results	
	9		20 rounds 6" fired at CORN TRENCH. Several direct hits	
			15 rounds 9.45" fired at M.G. emplacements. Good results	
	10		28 rounds 6" fired in accordance with R.I.A. programme	
			6 rounds 9.45 fired in accordance with programme. Starting 9.00 T.	
	11		32 rounds 6" fired at wire on RAILWY 6.15- T.M.D.A. from 6d and 2" D.A.	
			Administration of batteries passed . CUTTING and one patrol on WHIP TRENCH	
			85 rounds 6" fired at wire in first part of new	
	12		Two gaps made	
			8 rounds 9.45" fired at APE TRENCH in retaliation	
			41 rounds 6" fired at WIBBLE and in retaliation firing	
	13		64 rounds 6" fired at enemy trench system & unnecessary party. Moon in fair't distance	
	14		83 rounds 9.6" fired in reply to S.O.S. signal and in retaliation - shoots T.M's.	
	15		25 rounds 6" fired at enemy wire and working parties	
	16		30 rounds 6" fired at wire and in retaliation to hostile T.M.s.	
	17		18 rounds 9.4.5" fired on shelters in JUNCTION COPSE. Shooting accurate weight & lamp	
	18		26 rounds 9.5" fired at wire and working parties in CANDY TRENCH. Good results	
			78 rounds 9.6" fired at enemy wire. Good results. — One direct hit on BOSCH S	
			accomplice. Plane through observations	
	19		110 rounds 9.6 fired at wire and in retaliation to enemy bombardment	
			Blown gap of about 15 yds. wide made possible	

Army Form C. 2118.

WAR DIARY
15th Divn Trench/Mortar Bde No II
INTELLIGENCE SUMMARY.
for December 1917

(Erase heading not required.)

Instructions regarding War Diaries and Intelligence Summaries are contained in F. S. Regs., Part II. and the Staff Manual respectively. Title pages will be prepared in manuscript.

Place: ROEUX.

Date 1917	Hour	Summary of Events and Information	Remarks and references to Appendices
Dec 20		97 rounds 9.6" fired at wire and in retaliation. Quantity of wire blown up.	
21		2 small gaps of about 5 yards each.	
22		150 rounds 9.5" bat wing and in retaliation. Two gaps.	
23		162 rounds 6" fired at enemy wire. Wire fairly damaged and several gaps visible. One of about 1½ yards, one of 2 yards	
24		87 rounds 9.6" fired at enemy trenches in retaliation to hostile T.M.s. Very effective.	
		11 rounds 9.45" fired at S.O.S. line.	
25		162 rounds 6" fired in registration and retaliation.	
		2 rounds 9.45" fired at APE	
		108 rounds 6" fired at BOSCHE POSTS in front line and at hostile T.M.s.	
		Six fires disappeared from T.M. emplacement and did not reappear.	
26		9 rounds 9.45" fired at T.M. emplacement.	
		56 rounds 6" fired at enemy wire and in retaliation	
27		13 rounds 9.45" fired at T.M. emplacements & hostile PEAVES.	
		78 rounds 6" fired at enemy wire and hostile T.M.s.	
28		79 rounds 6" fired at enemy wire and working party. Wire badly damaged.	
29		28 rounds 6" fired at hostile T.M.s in WIBBLE & WHIP TRENCHES.	
30		84 rounds 6" fired in retaliation to hostile T.M.s.	
31		2 rounds 9.45" fired	
		112 rounds 6" fired at T.M. emplacements and in retaliation to enemy T.M.s.	

W. Scott. Capt.
15ᵗʰ D.T.M.B.

15TH DIVISION
TRENCH MORTAR
BRIGADE.
No. ....
Date 31-12-1917

Army Form C. 2118.

WAR DIARY
15.th Divn 2nd Trench Mortar Bde
INTELLIGENCE SUMMARY. January 1918

(Erase heading not required.)

Instructions regarding War Diaries and Intelligence Summaries are contained in F. S. Regs., Part II. and the Staff Manual respectively. Title pages will be prepared in manuscript.

Place	Date	Hour	Summary of Events and Information	Remarks and references to Appendices
ROEUX	1-1-18		63 rounds 6" fired at suspected T.M. emplacements and for retaliation.	
	2-1-18		82 rounds 6" fired in retaliation to enemy T.Ms.	
	3-1-18		Refitting guns and cleaning up of positions and guns preparatory to handing over.	
	4-1-18	10:30 am	Relieved by the Guards Divn Trench Mortar Bde.	
			Marched to DUISANS rest camp.	
DUISANS	5-1-18		Cleaning up camp. Inspection of men's kit and clothing.	
LIGNY ST FLOCHEL	6-1-18 to 19-1-18		Party of 100 consisting of Officers, N.C.O's and men proceeded to Ligny St Flochel III Army School of Mortars for Course of Instruction.	
DUISANS	20-1-18 to 24-1-18		Party of 15 O.R. to 15th D.A.C for fatigues. Physical Training, Musketry, Marching & Recreational Training	
BLANGY	25-1-18 to 31-1-18		Party proceeded to BLANGY for preparing reserve gun positions. Personnel left behind visited rifle range for firing purposes	
DUISANS				

15.th DIVISION
TRENCH MORTAR
BRIGADE.
31-1-18

O.S.Willis, Capt
15th D.T.M.B

CONFIDENTIAL.

WAR DIARY

of

15th Divisional Trench Mortar Brigade

Volume 14.

From 1st February 1918.   To 1st March 1918.

Army Form C. 2118.

WAR DIARY
15th Divⁿ Trench Mortar B.Sc.
INTELLIGENCE SUMMARY.— February 1918.
(Erase heading not required)

Place	Date February	Hour	Summary of Events and Information	Remarks and references to Appendices
DUISANS	1-2-18 to 6-2-18		Brigade was in rest billets. Physical training, musketry and machine gun drill carried out. Fatigue parties supplied for preparation of reserve positions.	
ARRAS. MONCHY LE PREUX	7		Brigade marched to ARRAS.	
	8		Took over positions in the line from 4th Divⁿ.	
	9		47 rounds 6" fired on S.O.S. lines during Artillery activity.	
	10		39 rounds 6" fired in retaliation to hostile T.M's. Trench Mortar B^{tie}s reorganised.	
	11		37 rounds 6" fired at hostile T.M's and for registration.	
	12		36 rounds 6" fired at hostile T.M's	
	13		33 rounds 6" fired for registration purposes on BOIS DU VERT.	
	14		12 rounds 6" fired for registration purposes on BOIS DU VERT.	
	15		34 rounds 6" fired in retaliation to hostile T.M's.	
	16		33 rounds 6" fired at enemy wire at junction of POWDER & DEVIL TRENCH.	
	17		58 rounds 6" fired at enemy niche and in retaliation to hostile T.M's.	
	18		40 rounds 6" fired at wire and in retaliation.	
	19		51 rounds 6" fired at enemy wire.	
	20		58 rounds 6" fired - 15 of these fired with aeroplane observation - Good results obtained.	
	21		50 rounds 6" fired at enemy wire making one gap of about 20 yards.	
	22		49 rounds 6" fired at hostile T.M's and at wire. Two large gaps cut about 15 yds wide.	
	23		64 rounds 6" fired in retaliation.	
	24		124 rounds 6" fired. 96 of these were fired during raid by 7th Cameronians.	
	25		52 rounds 6" fired at Enemy wire and in retaliation to hostile T.M's.	
	26		39 rounds 6" fired at wire. Shooting evato owing to high wind.	
	27		80 rounds 6" fires at enemy wire and hostile T.M's.	
	28		97 rounds 6" fired at wire. Gap of about 12 yards cut.	
			100 rounds 6" fired at wire and in retaliation. One gap evident.	

A. Wilson Capt
15^t D.T.M.O.

15th Divisional Artillery.

L

15th DIVISIONAL TRENCH MORTAR BRIGADE

MARCH 1918

Army Form C. 2118.

WAR DIARY
15th DIV" ar Trench Mortar BSc
INTELLIGENCE SUMMARY
March 1918

(Erase heading not required.)

Instructions regarding War Diaries and Intelligence Summaries are contained in F.S. Regs., Part II. and the Staff Manual respectively. Title pages will be prepared in manuscript.

Place	Date March	Hour	Summary of Events and Information	Remarks and references to Appendices
Monchy	1		64 rounds 6" fired at wire and enemy wiring party. Gap of about 10 yards made and wiring party dispersed leaving material behind.	
	2		16 rounds 6" fired in retaliation to hostile T.M.s.	
	3		44 rounds 6" fired in retaliation to hostile T.M.S.	
	4		54 rounds 6" fired in retaliation to hostile T.M.S.	
	5		42 rounds 6" fired in retaliation to hostile T.M.S.	
	6		156 rounds 6" fired for registration and in support of Inf. raid, in accordance with programme.	
	7		41 rounds 6" fired at enemy wire. Direct hit. Gap made of about 15 yds.	
	8		87 rounds 6" fired at enemy wire and in retaliation. Gaps increased.	
	9		139 rounds 6" fired during raid in accordance with programme.	
	10		60 rounds 6" fired at enemy wire. Further damage caused and several small gaps made.	
	11		109 rounds 6" fired at enemy T.M.s during raid in accordance with programme.	
	12		34 rounds 6" fired at enemy wire and in retaliation to T.M. T.M.S.	
	13		2 rounds 6" fired at enemy wire. Further firing impossible owing to weather.	
			50 rounds 6" fired at enemy wire with good effect. Dumps in HAPPY VALLEY fired by enemy fire.	
			56 rounds 6" fired at enemy wire. Wire considerably broken and 2 small gaps made.	
			Reserve personnel moved into huts at T.N.O.4. 30 Offrs, ranks attached from 15th D.A.C.	
			80 rounds 6" fired at wire and 5 enemy Trench Mortar lines. Wire considerably damaged and 6 Bosches seen to leave trenches.	
			93 rounds 6" fired at enemy wire. Enemy has been connecting up previous gaps with concertina wire. Gaps were reopened and numerous Bosch Gap't mats - numbers of enemy seen to leave trench mines - examined. These were sniped at.	

CONFIDENTIAL.

WAR DIARY

of

15th Divisional Trench Mortar Brigade.

(Volume 15.)

From 1st March 1918.   to 31st March 1918.

Army Form C. 2118.

WAR DIARY
15th Div - Trench Mortar Bde
INTELLIGENCE SUMMARY. March 1918

Vol 22

Place	Date March	Hour	Summary of Events and Information	Remarks and references to Appendices
MONCHY	18		101 rounds 6" fired at enemy wire - Gaps further increased and three small gaps made.	
	19		43 rounds 6" fired at enemy wire - Considerable amount broken and one new gap made.	
	20		62 rounds 6" fired at enemy wire in order to keep existing gaps open	
	21		36 rounds 6" fired at trench junctions in enemy system of trenches.	
	22		12 to S.O.S.	
	23		12 rounds 6" fired at S.O.S. targets. Personnel and guns removed from line to Brigade HQ in PRRAS during night in accordance with withdrawal scheme.	
	24		Direct hit obtained on Brigade HQ in PRRAS during today. Two men wounded. Brigade HQ's moved to new billet. Fatigue party sent to line to prepare fresh positions and carry ammunition. Eleven casualties occurred. 2 complete guns sent to line.	
	25		Work on new gun positions continued and one and 25 gun sent to line to line.	
	26		Work on gun positions continued.	
	27		Work on gun positions continued.	
	28		Enemy attacked. All personnel sent up to assist Infantry. 2 O.R. wounded 5 and 1 Officer and 11 O.R.s missing.	
	29		Men in lines with Infantry reserves and parties sent to guard dumps.	
	30		All personnel sent to Brigade O.C. wounded.	
	31		Onwards a company sent to line and two parties of men sent to R.F.A. Brigades for attachment.	

A.C.Wick Kapt.
18/3/1918

A854 Wt. W4973/M687 750,000 8/16 D. D. & L. Ltd Forms/C.2118/13

15th Divisional Artillery

WAR DIARY

15th Divisional TRENCH MORTAR BRIGADE

APRIL 1918

CONFIDENTIAL.

WAR DIARY

of

15th Divisional Trench Mortar Brigade

(Volume 16.)

From 1st April 1918.　　　　　　　　　　　　**To 30th April 1918.**

Army Form C. 2118.

WAR DIARY
15th Divl. Trench Mortar Bde
INTELLIGENCE SUMMARY for April

Vol 23

Place	Date April	Hour	Summary of Events and Information	Remarks and references to Appendices
ARRAS.	1		Party proceeded to line to prepare gun positions. Surplus personnel take to 15th D.A.C.	
	2		Work on position in line completed. Guns and ammunition conveyed to line.	
	3		6-6" fired at old Bridge S.A.A.s in enemy line. Gun put in action	
	4		14 rounds fired at old Battery positions and S.A.A.s in enemy line.	
	5		Guns withdrawn from line - 1 Offr. wounded.	
	6		Personnel attached Field Arty. Bdes. & D.A.C. rejoined. Guns brought up from D.A.C. Fresh positions reconnoitred in rear system.	
	7		Personnel on Ammunition Dump where Party proceeds to line for construction of gun emplacements.	
	8		Work on gun emplacements continued. 3 complete guns and sub. Bdes sent to line.	
	9		Work in line continued.	
	10.		One gun in action. Work on other emplacements continued.	
	11.		16 Reinforcements joined from 15th D.A.C. Work in line continued.	
	12&13		Work in line continued.	
	14		Headquarters and personnel moved to south side of ARRAS.	
	15.		3 guns and 5 sub. Bdes sent to line.	
	16-28		Work on reserve emplacements continued and detachments posted at completed positions.	
	29.		Positions in line taken over by 56th Divl. T.M.Bde.	
	30.	12:30pm	Brigade proceeded to Mont St-Eloi for entraining in accordance with 15th D.A. Marching Programme.	
		2:30pm	Orders for entraining cancelled. Bde. returned to billets in ARRAS.	

O.C. West Capt.
15th D.T.M.B

CONFIDENTIAL.

WAR DIARY

of

15th Divisional Trench Mortar Brigade.

(Volume 17.).

From 1st May 1918.

To 31st May 1918.

Army Form C. 2118.

WAR DIARY
15th Div" Trench Mortar B.Se
INTELLIGENCE SUMMARY
for May 1918

(Erase heading not required)

Place	Date May	Hour	Summary of Events and Information	Remarks and references to Appendices
ARRAS	1-2		Batteries standing to awaiting marching orders and cleaning guns. X Battery marched to camp of 4th Can. D.T.M.B.Se at Ecurie and detachments	
	3		proceeded there to take over guns.	
	4		Y Battery marched to camp of 4th Can. D.T.M.B.Se relief of whom was completed.	
	5-8		Cleaned and tidied up guns and positions. Camp cleaned and reasigned pos-	
	9		3-6" guns taken over in time from 2nd Div" T.M.B.Se. 3-6" guns handed over to	
	10-11		52nd Div" T.M.B.Se.	
	12-13		Improvements carried out at new positions.	
			Detachments in trenches standing to. Resting personnel on gun drill & musketry.	
	23		3 rounds 6" fired for registration of enemy M.G.	
	24-26		Detachments in trenches standing to. Resting personnel on gun drill.	
	27		9 rounds 6" fired in retaliation to enemy barrage fire.	
	28-29		Constructed 3 new emplacements and moved guns.	
	30		1/15 T.M.Bty. carried out infantry trial.	
	31		20 rounds 6" fired on hostile M.Gs at request of Infantry.	

A Sullivan Capt
15 D.T.M.O

CONFIDENTIAL.

WAR DIARY

OF

15th Divisional Trench Mortar Brigade

(volume 18.)

From 1st June 1918.   To 30th June 1918.

WAR DIARY

15th Divl. Trench Mortar Bde.

INTELLIGENCE SUMMARY

1st – 30th June 1918

Army Form C. 2118.

Place	Date June	Hour	Summary of Events and Information	Remarks and references to Appendices
	1		Cleaning up gun positions	
	2		2 rounds 6" fired at suspected enemy posts.	
	3		Experiments carried out with new stabilised	
	4		Probability Fuze by X/15 T.M. By.	
	5		Experiments carried out with new sub. Std.	
	6		Firing Tests carried out with new Std.	
	7-8		Musketry and marching drill	
	9		10 rounds 6" fired in reply to S.O.S. signal	
	10		Ammunition carrying in lieu to firing	
	15		positions	
	16		up to establishment	
	17		Positions taken over by 51st Divl. T.M.B.Sa. Batteries marched to ACQ.	
	18-19		Overhauling equipment and stores	
	20		Batteries march to ANZIN - Relieves 2nd Divl. T.M.B.Se in line at ATHIES.	
	21		Sidings and improving positions in line	
	22		Headquarters and Batteries moved to new billet	
	23		One gun moved from defenders to Forward Position	
	24		34 rounds 6" fired at enemy T.M. during raid.	
	25		Improvements carried out at gun positions	
	26		Y Battery relieved X Bty in line.	
	27-28		Fatigue party sent to BLANGY for cable burying fatigue.	
	29-30		Cleaning guns	

VR 25

Return 6th?
15th D.T.M.B.

CONFIDENTIAL.

WAR DIARY

OF

15th Divisional Trench Mortar Brigade.

(Volume 19.)

From 1st July 1918.

To 31st July 1918.

Army Form C. 2118.

WAR DIARY
15th Div. Trench Mortar Bde
INTELLIGENCE SUMMARY. for July 1918

Vol 26

(Erase heading not required.)

Instructions regarding War Diaries and Intelligence Summaries are contained in F. S. Regs., Part II. and the Staff Manual respectively. Title pages will be prepared in manuscript.

Place	Date July	Hour	Summary of Events and Information	Remarks and references to Appendices
ARRAS.	1		Ⓧ Preparing new gun positions	
	2		Y Battery relieved in line.	
	3-4		Preparing new gun positions and carrying ammunition	
	5		20 rounds 6" fired at enemy wire	
	6		20 rounds 6" fired at enemy wire	
	7		25 rounds 6" fired at enemy wire and buildings	
	8		X Battery relieved in line. Detachment march to LA CONTE	
	9		Detachment carrying out rifle trials at LA CONTE. 13 rounds 6" fired during trial. 10 rounds 6" also used.	
	10		21 rounds 6" fired at houses and enemy trenches.	
	11-13		Carrying ammunition.	
	14		2-6" T.Ms taken over from 56th Divn T.M. Bde.	
	15		Brigade relieved by 1st Can Divn. T.M. Bde. Personnel marched to AGNIÈRES.	
AUBIGNY	16		Preparing for entrainment	
	17		Brigade entrained at AUBIGNY.	
BRENOUILLE	18		X Bty detrained at LIANCOURT. Y Bty detrained at CLERMONT. Brigade marched to BRENOUILLE	
VERBERIE	19		Standing to awaiting orders	
VAUX-MOULIN	20		Brigade marched to VERBERIE.	
COEUVRES	21		Proceeded by lorries to VAUX MOULIN	
	22		X Bty proceeded to COEUVRES. Party sent to D.A.C. Dump.	
	23		Y Bty proceeded to COEUVRES. Party sent to D.A.C. Dump.	
	24-31		Ammunition fatigues at D.A.C. Dump.	
	27		Traffic post established at BEAUREPAIRE FARM.	
	29		Three men sent to 27th M.V.S.	
	30.		Men at Traffic post relieved.	

W.D. Garrett Capt.
for 15th D.T.M.O.

CONFIDENTIAL.

WAR DIARY

of

15th Divisional Trench Mortar Brigade

From 1st August 1918.   To 31st August 1918.

(Volume 20).

Army Form C. 2118

WAR DIARY
15th Div. "Trench Mortar" Bde
INTELLIGENCE SUMMARY for August 1918

(Erase heading not required.)

Instructions regarding War Diaries and Intelligence Summaries are contained in F. S. Regs., Part II. and the Staff Manual respectively. Title Pages will be prepared in manuscript.

VR 27

Place	Date August 1918	Hour	Summary of Events and Information	Remarks and references to Appendices
COEUVRES	1		Fatigue parties provided to salve cable.	
	2-4		Clearing up Dumps for D.A.C.	
	5		X-Battery proceeded to LIANCOURT by lorry - Y Battery proceeded to CLERMONT by lorry.	
	6		X-Battery entrained at LIANCOURT - Y Battery entrained at CLERMONT.	
HOUVIN-HOUVIGNEUL	7		Brigade arrived at TINQUES and marched to HOUVIN-HOUVIGNEUL.	
	8-12		Inspection of kit and equipment. Cleaning guns.	
	13-15		Physical training, marching and recreational training.	
	16		Brigade proceeded to SIMENCOURT by lorry.	
	17		Relieved 56th Div. T.M. Bde in line.	
	18		Cleaning up gun positions.	
ARRAS	19		Headquarters proceeded to ARRAS.	
	20-24		Detachments on guns in line "standing to".	
	25-27		Fatigue parties provided for road making during advance. Men attached to R.F.A. Bde for signal work during operations.	
	28		Removing guns from emplacements in line. Headquarters proceeded to WANCOURT.	
	29		Guns conveyed from line to near headquarters.	
	30		Salving ammunition at old emplacements.	
	31		Cleaning up guns and equipment.	

M15 Garrett Capt
for 15th D.T.M.B.

CONFIDENTIAL.

W A R   D I A R Y

of

15th Divisional Trench Mortar Brigade

(Volume 21)

From 1st September 1918.　　　　To 30th September 1918.

WAR DIARY

15th Divn Trench Mortar Bde

INTELLIGENCE SUMMARY

for September 1918

Army Form C. 2118.

Place	Date 1918 Sept	Hour	Summary of Events and Information	Remarks and references to Appendices
WANCOURT	1-4		Fatigue parties supplies by Salving Ammunition - making roads during attack, and assisting Sappers.	
ARRAS	5		Fatigue parties relieved by 50th Divn T.M.B&e	
HERSIN	6		Proceeded by lorry from ARRAS to HERSIN.	
	7		Guns and equipment cleaned.	
NOYELLES	8		X Battery proceeded to NOYELLES by lorry and relieved 11th Divn T.M.B&s in rest.	
	9		Y Battery proceeded to rear HQrs NOYELLES	
	10		Billets cleaned and rearranged.	
	11	13 rounds 6" fired at O.P. on STAG HEAP	
	12	113 rounds 6" fired at request of infantry.	
	13	moving guns to new positions	
	14	23 rounds 6" fired in reply to S.O.S. Signal - X Battery relieving in line by Y Battery	
	15	93 rounds 6" fired at trench junctions and in retaliation to hostile T.M.s at request of infantry Commanders.	
	16	Carrying ammunition to forward positions.	
	17	164 rounds 6" fired at selected targets during daylight raid by infantry.	
	18	moving guns to forward positions.	
	19	55 rounds 6" fired at hostile T.M.s and at trench junctions during raids.	
	20	5 rounds 6" fired in reply to S.O.S. - Y Battery relieved in line by X Battery.	
	21	20 rounds 6" fired at hostile T.M.s.	
	22	Carrying Ammunition to trench positions.	
	23	14 rounds 6" fired at hostile T.M.s and at enemy wire during gas projector attack.	
	24	33 rounds 6" fired at junctions of enemy trenches.	
	25	54 rounds 6" fired at enemy trenches in retaliation to hostile T.M. & B&y shelling by Y B&y	
	26	17 rounds 6" fired on hostile T.M.s with 2 aeroplanes observing. The battery was completely obliterated.	
	27	34 rounds 6" fired at supports and hostile T.M. emplacement. The battery only suffered considerable damage caused to registered T.M.	
	28	149 rounds 6" fired in direct support of numerous operations & registrations. Numerous gaps were cleared in enemy wire at cutting operations & registrations.	
	29	213 rounds 6" fired in Syst of X B&y 9 inf in support of raid by infantry.	
	30	249 rounds 6" fired at hostile T.M.	
		5 rounds 6" fired at hostile T.M.	

Lens & Hulluch Sectors.

Vol 29.

CONFIDENTIAL

War Diary
of
15th Divisional T. M. Bde.

From 1/10/18 to 31/10/18

Volume 22.

Army Form C. 2118.

WAR DIARY
of 15th Division French Mor/Sg. Bde.
INTELLIGENCE SUMMARY.
For October 1918

(Erase heading not required)

Instructions regarding War Diaries and Intelligence Summaries are contained in F.S. Regs., Part II. and the Staff Manual respectively. Title pages will be prepared in manuscript.

Place	Date OCTOBER	Hour	Summary of Events and Information	Remarks and references to Appendices
LOOS	1		26 rounds 86 fired on neo and on request of infantry.	
	2		Carried ammunition to forward positions.	
	3		Battery to men's ground forward.	
	4,5		Y Battery relieved by X Battery.	
VENIN	6		Moving by platoons to new S. positions.	
	7		2 rounds 86 fired at targets TMS.	
	8		Headquarters moved to LOOS. 10 rounds 86 fired at occupied houses in GIVENCHY.	
	9		15 rounds 86 found at occupied houses.	
	10		10 rounds 86 firing for registration.	
	11		20 rounds 86 fired at occupied houses at request of infantry.	
	12		30 rounds 86 fired at M.G. nests and other buildings.	
	13		68 rounds 86 fired at enemy posts and houses. TMS.	
	14		17 rounds 86 fired at suspected T.M. and M.G. emplacements. TMS.	
			38 rounds 86 fired at houses and enemy TMS.	
MEUCHIN	15		Small field trench mortars crossed RIV'R DEULE on 96 temporary and fixed MEUCHIN.	
	16		Batty mortars moved to FOSSE 2.	
NEUVILLE	17		Batty mortars marched from L. CARVIN RUGEN Construlid temporary crossing over railway m.5.	
NOUVEAU-JEU	18		Ready for action at NOUVEAU JEU. Headquarters moved to RUMLEY.	
GENECH	19		Amhd Mortars preceded to GENECH and continued to LA PLEZ in the evening.	
TOUPET	20		Headquarters moved to MASNIERES.	
			Small mortars moved by lighter from MASNIERES to BELGIAN frontier and R.T.A. B.de. Cadre of B.G.B. L. Hon. Art. Major Morris in detona at TOUPET Fired from detonat.	
GUIGNIES	21		at Langemark to GUIGNIES.	
	22/23		Small mortars marched to GUIGNIES. Headquarters marched to MOUCHIN.	
	24		Marching line.	
	25		One mortar and ammunition sent forward with detachment to KERLIN.	
	26		Remaining line. 1 to PETIT RUMES.	
WEZ VELVAN	27		Artillery marches to WEZ VELVAN.	
	28		Y Batty marches WEZ VELVAN.	
	29		Remaining line.	
	30			
	31		Overhauling guns and equipment.	

O.C. Slick

Capt. J.
15th D.M.B.

CONFIDENTIAL.

WAR DIARY.

of

15th Divisional Trench Mortar Brigade.

(Volume 23.)

From 1st November 1918.   To 30th November 1918.

Army Form C. 2118.

WAR DIARY
15th Dvn. Trench Mortar Bty.
INTELLIGENCE SUMMARY.

November 1918

(Erase heading not required.)

Instructions regarding War Diaries and Intelligence Summaries are contained in F. S. Regs., Part II. and the Staff Manual respectively. Title pages will be prepared in manuscript.

Place	Date	Hour	Summary of Events and Information	Remarks and references to Appendices
VELAIN	November 1918 1		Lecture on Ammunition.	
	2		Lecture on Lewis Gun and demonstration.	
	3		Reconnoitring Line.	
	4-5		Lecture on Gas and Anti-Gas measures.	
	6-7		Cleaning guns and ammunition.	
BRUYELLE	8		Battery marched to BRUYELLE. Two mobile guns placed in action and 23rd 15 fired.	
ANTOING	9		Headquarters marched to ANTOING.	
BRAIGNIES	10		Headquarters marched to BRAIGNIES.	
	11		X Battery marched to BRAIGNIES.	
	12		Headquarters marched to MOULBAIX.	
MOULBAIX	13		Brigade marched to CHIÈVRES.	
CHIÈVRES	14		Gun attd. to 71st Bde. R.F.A. to replace casualties.	
	15		Bty attd. for rations to 15th D.A.C.	
	16-20		Cleaning and oiling guns and equipment.	
	21		Parties formed from T.M. Bde R.F.A and 15th D.A.C.	
	22-24		Drill Parades and recreation ab. training.	
	25		Inspection parties returned to R.A.O.S.	
	26		Brigade inspected by G.O.C. Division.	
	27		Educational Classes commenced.	
	28		Foundry Parade and Battalion Demobilisation.	
	29-30		Classes, Rifle Drill and Recreational Training.	

W.S. Elliott. Capt.
15th D.T.M.B.

CONFIDENTIAL.

WAR DIARY

of

15th Divisional Trench Mortar Brigade.

(Volume 24.)

From 1st December 1918.   To 31st December 1918.

Army Form C. 2118.

WAR DIARY
15th Div: French Mob: Bde
INTELLIGENCE SUMMARY.
1st December 1918.

(Erase heading not required.)

VII 31

Place	Date Dec	Hour	Summary of Events and Information	Remarks and references to Appendices
CHIEVRES	1-10		Men attached to Field Artillery Brigades for fatigues. Personnel left employed on harness cleaning Brill, Rifle Drill, Educational exercises and Recreational training.	
MOULBAIX	11		Brigade marches to MOULBAIX	
	12		Party attached D.A.C. for fatigues.	
	13-15		Overhauling equipment and cleaning guns.	
TONGRE NOTRE DAME	16		Brigade marches to TONGRE NOTRE DAME	
HORRUES	17		Brigade marches to HORRUES	
REBECQ	18		Brigade marches to REBECQ.	
	19		Story arrived at REBECQ.	
	20-29		Parties supplied for fatigues at coal dump, D.A.G. Supply dump.	
	30 31		Artillery baths and guards supplied for coal dumps. Party sent to B.A.C.	

A. White Capt.
15th D.M.D

CONFIDENTIAL.

WAR DIARY.

of

15th Divisional Trench Mortar Brigade.

(Volume 25.)

From 1st January 1919.

To 31st January 1919.

Army Form C. 2118.

WAR DIARY
or
INTELLIGENCE SUMMARY.
(Erase heading not required.)

JANUARY. 1919.

Instructions regarding War Diaries and Intelligence Summaries are contained in F. S. Regs., Part II. and the Staff Manual respectively. Title pages will be prepared in manuscript.

No 32

Place	Date	Hour	Summary of Events and Information	Remarks and references to Appendices
REBECQ- ROGNON.	1st to 31st		During this period T.M personnel has been employed in fatigues - Guns Stores etc have been the overhauled.	

A.Chinn t Capt
for DTMO

CONFIDENTIAL.

WAR DIARY

of

15th Divisional Trench Mortar Brigade.

(Volume 26)

From 1st February 1919.   To 28th February 1919.

Army Form C. 2118.

WAR DIARY

15 Div Tren or Mortar Bat.

INTELLIGENCE SUMMARY.

(Erase heading not required.)

Place	Date	Hour	Summary of Events and Information	Remarks and references to Appendices
Reberg Rognon	15/6 /4 /17		Cleaning and oiling Lewis and equipment. 2 men attached to 15 Div M.G. Bn at no Goderly. 4 men joined YOX B60 RFA act is mount over railway trucks. Henry Yseros Station. 3 men took M.M.Q. tards a Chrudy. all remaining men and officers to go 15 D.A.C. board 15 D.A.C. 4 men remaining on as orders.	

J.W. Symons Lt
for OC
15 D.T.M.O

www.ingramcontent.com/pod-product-compliance
Lightning Source LLC
Chambersburg PA
CBHW081556160426
43191CB00011B/1948